CONTENTS

book gives a broad coverage of most aspects of the war but the emphasis of the Study Guide and the DVD is largely on Britain's experience of the war and the way it was viewed by those who lived through it.

People's war(s)

WW2 People's War is the title of the BBC project which deals with the experience of the people who lived through World War 2 and seeks to recapture their war-time lives by inviting them to respond online. Such 'oral' evidence (for the term covers the recording by any means of personal recollections) from those remembering and reminiscing long afterwards adds to the long list of sources we have to draw on for the Second World War and we shall make use of some extracts in this guide. In addition to central primary sources such as diplomatic documents and the letters and speeches of statesmen, we have rich material that is particularly useful for evaluating war-time attitudes: the diaries and autobiographies, not just of statesmen and generals, but of Land Army women, evacuated children, soldiers and factory workers; radio archives; documentary and feature films of the period; and museums, like the Imperial War Museum, with their collections of everything from tanks and planes to ration books.

Oral evidence, whether we are dealing with words spoken at the time either in the form of recordings or transcripts or with recollections of the time, is a rich source for the historian. The evidence of individuals about their own experiences, whether in the form of oral history or diaries and memoirs, provides a useful means of reconstructing the attitudes and opinions of the British public during World War 2. This is particularly useful, perhaps, for uncovering the feelings and experiences of those whose voices would otherwise not be heard. In this Study Guide, we make use of a number of personal accounts and reactions both *from* the time and from recollections *of* the time.

Like all historical sources, however, personal accounts have their advantages and their snares. How, for instance, do we know whether accounts and reactions given at the time represented what people thought, or what they thought they should say? Are memories recollected decades after events adjusted to fit the picture of the events given by books or TV programmes? All sources need to be placed in context and can be sometimes as significant for what they don't say, and what we find significant, as well as for what the writers or speakers of the time thought significant.

Whether we can ever really know and understand the past, even the recent past and even the past that we ourselves have lived in, is a question that historians perennially debate. When it comes to the experience of the British people in the Second World War, we certainly can't complain about lack of evidence and, as the collective memory of the war is an important part of our identity, the attempt to understand and to get inside this particular past is more than worthwhile.

Let us not, however, underestimate the difficulties. We can walk inside the '1940s House' in the Imperial War Museum, just as we can visit a regency mansion, furnished as at the time it was built, but we haven't the assumptions or the mind set of the 1940s any more than those of the 1810s. For those of us over a certain age this is the sort of kitchen we had and this is the kind of wireless on which we listened to a programme such as *Workers' Playtime*, but can we really recapture that world? Perhaps perversely, the greater familiarity of the more recent past, especially for those of us who lived during the period, can be misleading.

Like most historians we consider that by carefully validating and questioning our sources, we can get close to knowing and understanding the past while accepting that there can never be one definitive account.

ACTIVITY

Now listen to Item 2, 'Sources', on the DVD. It is a discussion about historical sources.

A people's war?

The term 'people's war' inevitably brings to mind the term using the definite article, '**the**' people's war. All wars have of course been fought by or between people but not necessarily by *peoples*. It was claimed by some contemporaries and has been asserted by some historians that the Second World War was for the British a 'people's war' in two particular senses: all of society was involved in the war effort and affected by it, young or old, men and women; and there was a strong sense of national unity and social cohesion. It's a term that's worth analysing for it is also sometimes associated with an egalitarian ethos, which, it has been argued, was born of common hardships and experiences.

It has been argued, notably by Arthur Marwick, Emeritus Professor of History at the Open University, that the great wars of the twentieth century were quintessentially different to previous wars because they were 'total wars' which involved not simply armies but entire populations in the war effort (see A. Marwick, *War and Social Change in the Twentieth Century* (1975)). The 'Home Front' and those working in factories, docks and farms were as important as those fighting at the front. In World War 2 bombing raids further eroded the distinctions between servicemen and civilians. To put this in context, 55,000 men of Bomber Command were killed on active service while some 60,000 British people died in air raids during the war.

In such circumstances it was vital to capture the support and maintain the morale of all sections of society. So it was necessary for the government to promote the notion of a people's war that not only encouraged everyone to 'do their bit', but would also respond to their hopes and aspirations for a better and more socially egalitarian society. The government department responsible for monitoring and maintaining morale, the Ministry of Information (MOI), produced a plethora of books, pamphlets and official films to support the idea that the war involved the entire population and had its whole-hearted support. Today we may question how far official propaganda (for that is what it was, despite the often pejorative connotations of the word) accurately reflected the wartime spirit. One of the things we will do in this study pack is to help you evaluate these sources and to question the extent to which they represent an authentic picture of British society during the war.

These are important questions, for the British are proud of their role in the Second World War, and this pride, mixed with some nostalgia, has played a significant part in allowing us to come to terms with the loss of the empire and of great power status since 1945. That Britain alone maintained the fight against Germany after the fall of France, that the population was firm and united in this stance and that there was moral excellence and courage in the way that a communal spirit informed the war effort and enabled both military and civilian hardships and casualties to be endured, are all central to a historical narrative that underpins our national self-image. A sense of a worthy and heroic communal past is intrinsic to the identity of nations and, if Agincourt, the Armada, Blenheim and Waterloo are major events in the British past, none play so great a part as the remembered glories of the more recent World War 2. In this popular version of history, the Second World War was for the British people, as Churchill put it, their 'finest hour'.

The still-hallowed version of Britain's role in World War 2, a version that combines the view of the war as another glorious chapter in British history with that of a democratic and egalitarian 'people's war' was in place even before 1945 and was largely uncontested for several decades after the war's end. Revisionism is, however, central to historical debate and it could not be expected that this account would remain unscathed: archival material, previously withheld, became available; younger historians who had not experienced the war looked at it with different eyes; while, as time passed, there were new perspectives and awkward questions. Was British society at war really so united? Did the war bring about the sort of far-reaching social change that some contemporaries believed was the case? Had the significance of Britain's role in the war been exaggerated? Was Churchill a great war-time leader or was he responsible for major mistakes? Were the much criticised appeasers actually correct in trying to prevent a war with Germany? Perhaps there had even been a case for reaching an understanding with Germany after the fall of France. The debate continues.

Now let us go back to the beginning, in so far as historical events and developments ever have a beginning.

WHY DID BRITAIN GO TO WAR IN 1939?

After reading Chapter 1 of *The Second World War*, you will be aware that the origins and causes of the war are by no means uncontroversial.

Now read Chapter 1 of *The Second World War*.

Then jot down a brief answer, in point form, to the following question (this should take approximately 10 minutes):

Why did Britain, along with France, declare war on Germany in September 1939?

COMMENT

A short and accurate, even if insufficient, answer is that Britain, followed by France, had given Poland a guarantee to do so and that the German invasion of Poland activated that guarantee. But we then have to ask why the western allies should have gone to war because of a dispute between Germany and Poland which ostensibly concerned Danzig, a town with a mainly German population, and which was not a matter of pressing concern to the British people.

Some of you may have opted for the more long-term view of the war's causes which holds that World War 2 was not really a separate war but rather a further round in a long war of the twentieth century which had started in 1914. This war had its origins in the emergence of a united Germany in 1871, which upset the prevailing balance of power in Europe and resulted in a strong state in the centre of Europe with ambitions for dominance and fears of encirclement. Defeated in World War 1, but left intrinsically strong by the Versailles Settlement, Germany persevered in its aim to become the predominant power in central Europe.

Even if we accept this, we have, however, to confront further questions. Could a different kind of peace settlement at the end of the First World War have led to a more stable Europe, solved the crucial problem of Germany's ambitions and prevented a second war or second round? The Versailles Settlement was arguably too harsh for Germany to be reconciled to its provisions and yet it left Germany potentially powerful. Its support for national self-determination left east-central Europe divided between mutually hostile states and, as peoples didn't fit frontiers, left many potential trouble spots.

Did the Versailles Settlement lead inescapably to a new war, or were there turning points between 1919 and 1939? Objections to the thesis that Versailles was responsible include the relative stability of Europe for some years after aspects of the peace treaty were modified by the Treaty of Locarno in 1925, and the fact that Germany had managed to overturn almost every article of Versailles to which it objected by 1939 (except for its claims to Danzig) without going to war.

Above all, there is the question of the importance of Adolf Hitler. That the war was all about Hitler remains the popular view of the war, and it may well be an accurate one. Whether or not Hitler had settled, long-term aims for world conquest, it is certainly true that his rise to power resulted in an increasingly aggressive German foreign policy. Most German politicians may have wished to overturn Versailles, but Hitler delighted in the threat of force and was prepared to take the risk of war.

How do historians evaluate the impact of Hitler or indeed of Hitler and Stalin? There have been complaints that the teaching of twentieth-century history is too dominated by the dictators – the 'men with moustaches'. Were they more important than the ideologies they represented? Conversely, were deep-seated national ambitions more significant than dictators or ideologies?

Others have seen the slide towards war as not so much the result of the problems posed by Hitler but as the result of the failure of the other great powers, and especially Britain and France, to stand up to Hitler. If only, it is argued, the western allies had stood firm when German troops broke the terms of the Versailles Settlement and re-occupied the Rhineland or had embarked upon rearmaments programmes earlier and more strenuously, then the crisis would have come earlier and Hitler would have been defeated before he became stronger or, alternatively, been removed by the German army.

In the end the British government declared war on Germany with great reluctance, feeling it had exhausted every peaceful stratagem for containing German ambitions and that essential British interests and the balance of power in Europe were threatened by those ambitions.

We now turn to the problems facing British governments in the 1930s and to British public opinion in so far as we can assess it.

PRE-WAR BRITAIN AND THE APPROACH OF WAR

On the accompanying DVD, we have included an item that was part of the Gaumont-British newsreel issued on 27 August 1936. Gaumont-British was one of five companies that held a virtual monopoly over the cinema newsreel industry. During the 1930s the twice-weekly newsreels were seen by between 15 and 19 million people a week and were second only to the radio as a source of news information for most British people.

ACTIVITY

Please now watch Item 3, '*The World Today*', on your DVD.
As you watch, bear in mind these questions:

1   What image does the newsreel present of the state and condition of Britain in 1936?

2   What position does the newsreel take on the question of appeasement?

COMMENT

1   Through both its commentary and its imagery, the newsreel presents Britain as a safe haven in an increasingly troubled world. Note how it contrasts problems elsewhere in the world, such as Abyssinia (invaded by Italy in 1935) and Spain (where a civil war had broken out in 1936), with a stable and secure Britain. There is a particular emphasis on British institutions, such as the police and the judiciary, and especially the monarchy. The commentary asserts that Edward VIII 'has proved a worthy successor to his great father and to his grandfather, Edward the Peacemaker'. (This is a reference to Edward VII, whose diplomacy in 1904 had been instrumental in the forging of the Entente Cordiale which went a long way towards healing enmities between Britain and France.) The references to 'Britain's industries

[arising] from the slough of despond' assert that manufacturing is on the road to recovery following the slump of the early 1930s. Furthermore, the newsreel reminds us, Britain is the centre of a great empire that extends all around the world. And it assures its audiences that Britain is protected by its armed forces, with the army, navy and air force providing security in response to the turmoil in Europe and elsewhere.

2   The commentary does not mention the word 'appeasement' specifically, of course, but you may have noticed this brief reference: 'Statesmen who may have drawn upon themselves criticism from time to time have nevertheless worked tirelessly for peace at home and abroad. As we look back we realise that their efforts have brought this country safely through the innumerable crises that have beset it in the past few years.' This seems an endorsement of the foreign policy of the National Government during the 1930s, which sought to resolve international disputes through peaceful means and negotiation rather than war.

Yet we might have reason to question the picture portrayed in this item (which was, originally, to have been called 'Wonderful Britain'). In the first place, the newsreels, for all that their editors clung to the mantra of independence, were generally inclined to support the government of the day. They chose and edited their stories in a way that implicitly endorsed the political and economic policies of the National Government. Indeed, the Labour Party complained that the favourable presentation of leading politicians such as Stanley Baldwin and Neville Chamberlain by the newsreels was a significant factor in the success enjoyed by the Conservatives in the general election of 1935.

Historians, furthermore, have cause to dispute the cosy picture of Britain presented here. It is not so apparent, for example, that British industry was recovering as successfully as the newsreel suggests. The rise of new industries such as motor car manufacturing, chemicals and electrical engineering to some extent masked the long-term structural decline of traditional industries such as ship-building and textile manufacturing, where unemployment remained severe throughout the 1930s. The monarchy, presented here as a unifying influence, would within a few months be rocked to its foundations by the Abdication Crisis. And, in strategic terms, the British government was less confident of its security than the reassuring image of battleships and aeroplanes on display here would suggest. The rebuilding of the German navy – exemplified in 1935 by the commissioning of the first of the so-called 'pocket battleships' (a term used by the British to describe ships that were, in effect, armoured cruisers with battleship-sized, i.e. 11-inch, guns) – represented a threat to British naval supremacy, while Stanley Baldwin's famous comment, as early as 1932, that 'the bomber will always get through', reflected contemporary fears that there would be no adequate defence against the new bombing planes.

So what was the state and condition of Britain in the 1930s? Britain was a great power with few ambitions, save to maintain its interests. For all that Britain had an extensive empire and the largest navy in the world, it was, nevertheless, a weak colossus, a great power which could not afford to go to war because by doing so it was likely to cease to be a great power.

To understand Britain either during the inter-war period or during the war, we must appreciate the centrality of the empire. Consciousness of the empire was an important part of British identity: Britain was not just a small island on Europe's periphery but was the centre of a large and varied empire. Most British food came from the empire, Britons celebrated Empire Day and much employment was generated, directly or indirectly by the empire. It was not just Britain which had fought the First World War and would fight the Second but the British Empire and Commonwealth, too. The empire was a unifying influence on British society, something of which all classes were proud.

However, British resources were insufficient to be able to defend the empire and to fight a war in Europe simultaneously. No one realised this more than Neville Chamberlain, who became Prime Minister in 1937. And perhaps no-one realised this *less* than Winston Churchill who, having held high office in governments since the Edwardian period, was a backbencher in the 1930s associated with lost causes, such as firm British control of the Indian Empire and support for King Edward VIII prior to his abdication. He was also associated with the not very popular cause of forthright opposition to Hitler and Mussolini. Chamberlain agonised over Britain's inherently weak position and was faced with a growing Japanese threat to the Empire in the Far East and Hitler's ambitions in Europe, while there were inadequate armed forces and the economy was struggling to escape from depression. Churchill, conversely, was sublimely confident that national will would enable Britain to take on Germany successfully.

ACTIVITY

Write a paragraph outlining a brief answer to the following question (this should take approximately 10 minutes):

What was the British public's opinion of going to war?

COMMENT

You may well have been cautious here and wondered whether there is such a thing as 'public opinion' rather than streams of opinion about lots of different matters. We could be on safer ground if we talk of the composite opinion of the majority on specific questions but even here there are difficulties because opinion is a slippery, contradictory and constantly changing creature. To assess it, whether in peace or war-time, is notoriously difficult. Alternatively, you may have stressed the great reluctance of much of the British public to be drawn into another war and referred to the support for Chamberlain, who, judging from the cheering crowds that greeted him on his return from Munich promising 'peace in our time', would seem to have had very substantial public support for his appeasement policy.

Today we have opinion polls and can supposedly take the national temperature every five minutes, though even such polls are fallible. For most of the pre-war period we have little opinion poll evidence. We do have, however, a mass of information about Britain and British society collected by government departments and by newspaper surveys as well as vast and varied sources, ranging from private papers to the literature of the time. A valuable source is the findings of the social survey organisation, Mass-Observation. Founded in 1937, Mass-Observation recruited unpaid volunteers to observe British society at work and play, and collated their reports. Not particularly scientific in its methods and with the observers largely self-selected or recruited haphazardly, the findings of Mass-Observation nevertheless provide unique insights into the opinions and mores of *some* of the British in the last years of peace and the years of war. In the end, however, in assessing British opinion we are in the world of informed but contestable generalisations.

There was a prevalent fear of another war among a broad swathe of British opinion. The Great War of 1914–18 was a recent memory; British losses had been heavy and Britain did not appear to have benefited from its costly victory. People knew that the machinery of warfare had become even more deadly since 1918. That there was a substantial body of near pacifist opinion was made manifest in the great number of signatures for the Peace Pledge Union. Many felt that preventing wars, dealing with aggression and settling disputes were matters for the League of Nations. It is difficult to quantify such attitudes or to decide how deep-seated they were but it certainly made support for re-armament programmes difficult for the government, especially as the view that armaments led to war was widely held.

It's also worth noting that it was more difficult for liberal-capitalist governments to prepare for war than it was for totalitarian regimes like

Hitler's next expansionary step. Whether this marked the end of appeasement or a modification of it, 'Appeasement with a big stick', but with the aim of a compromise over Hitler's demands on Poland, is debatable. Fear of war remained but most people seem to have begun to accept that war might be necessary.

For two sections of British opinion, those on the far right and far left, the events of 1939 were awkward. Members of the British Union of Fascists and those who saw fascism and national socialism as positive influences had to choose between their proclaimed patriotism and the fact that Germany and Italy seemed the enemies of Britain. Communist Party members and many other socialists to the left of the Labour Party saw the Soviet Union as the model for the future and the hope of the world. The policy recommended to them from Moscow in 1938 and the first half of 1939 was an anti-fascist popular front, a policy which had been hardened by the Spanish Civil War. Then, in August 1939, came the news of the Hitler–Stalin Pact. The two sworn enemies had come together and agreed among other things on the partition of Poland (see Figure 1). After Britain and France declared war on Germany on 3 September, the new Soviet doctrine transmitted to communist parties throughout the world was that this was a war between imperialists, and communists need not take sides.

Figure 1   *Rendezvous*, 20 September, 1939 (*Source*: Low, *Europe Since Versailles: A History in One Hundred Cartoons with a Narrative Text*, Harmondsworth, Penguin, 1940, p.207)

The British public, or the majority of it, grimly accepted the declaration of war made known to them, at 11.00 am on Sunday 3 September 1939, in a broadcast by the Prime Minister. We have included this broadcast on your DVD.

Listen now to Item 5, 'Declaration of war', on your DVD.

Many people were at the breakfast table and almost everyone, it is said, remembered for the rest of their lives where they were when they heard this broadcast.

A female National Panel diarist for Mass-Observation wrote:

A momentous day

11–11.15 a.m.

The Prime Minister is about to break the news of the war. It is inevitable. I have been convinced of it since last September. Hope against hope for peace, impossible with the greed and evilness of humanity spreading.

War, – how ghastly…

(Calder and Sheridan, *Speak for Yourself*, 1984, p.163)

A woman who was a child at the time recollected that:

It was Sunday morning soon after my seventh birthday. What was so important about 11 o'clock? My parents were talking in undertones. Mary and Bob from the flat below were coming upstairs from the flat below to listen to the radio.

'Hush no talking,' to my two-year-old sister and myself.

(BBC *WW2 People's War*, Joan Stokoe)

For Londoners the message of the broadcast was driven home by the air-raid siren (it turned out to be a false alarm) that went off shortly afterwards:

Within half an hour of the announcement and of being at war, the warning siren, which we had previously heard in practice, sounded its dreadful ominous undulating wail. Surely not, they can't be coming already, and with uncertainty and not quite sure what action to take, we all went to the window. The siren had stopped and the road outside was deserted apart from two middle-aged gentlemen who were running like the wind...

(BBC *WW2 People's War*, Bill Clavey)

A young woman in Northumberland who was an amateur pilot and later became a pilot in the Air Transport Auxiliary recollected a different reaction:

The Sunday that war was declared, I went out to a lunch party and I remember that it was mainly women, because all the chaps had gone to get on with things. I can remember quite clearly the butler coming in with his silver salver, bowing low from the waist and making an announcement to the effect that the Germans were already invading the country. The lady of the house was dishing out raspberry fool, I think it was, and she paused for a minute with the spoon in mid-air and said, 'Thank you L – .' and then sat down and continued as if nothing had happened.

(Jane Torday, *Wish Me Luck As You Wave Me Goodbye*, 1989, p.157)

ACTIVITY

Give brief answers to the following questions (spend only about 10 minutes on this):

1 Why did the British think they had gone to war?

2 What did people feel they were fighting for?

COMMENT

One could, of course, argue that we don't know and/or that there were a variety of opinions, which included those who were against the war.

You probably noted that the question is rather different to 'Why did Britain go to war?' to which *The Second World War* suggests the answer that it was 'to prevent a German domination of Europe'. You might have answered 'to stop Hitler'. In fact there was probably not much difference between the government's reasons for war and majority popular feeling.

We would suggest that what evidence we have of contemporary opinion suggests a 'Here we go again' feeling. This was another war against Germany. To a degree Germany was personified as Hitler but then there was plenty of evidence that Hitler was popular in Germany. Some, though probably a smallish minority, thought in terms of a war against fascism. Nazi policy towards the Jews was generally disapproved of but was not a factor in either the government's decision to go to war or majority support for it. The public were well aware that the German invasion of Poland was the occasion for war but that the reason for Britain's intervention was to prevent a German domination of Europe.

To hark back to our previous point about the importance of the empire, we should note that it was not just Britain which declared war on Germany along with France, but Britain and the British Empire. For the directly governed colonies, joining in the war was automatic, but all the self-governing dominions (even, by a narrow parliamentary vote, South Africa) followed Britain's lead.

BRITAIN'S WAR

Britain (here we include in this term the British Empire and Commonwealth) was the only Allied power that went to war in 1939 and remained an undefeated combatant until the defeat of Germany in 1945. This gives Britain's war a singularity and a timescale, 1939–45, shared only with its opponent, Germany. In the war against Japan, which began in December 1941 and ended in August 1945, Britain was the only European power to play a major role.

ACTIVITY

Now read Chapter 2 of *The Second World War*.

Thus, there is a special and peculiar British perspective of the war that differs from those of its shifting European allies and of the USA. It evokes comparisons with previous wars, such as the French Revolutionary and Napoleonic wars, when Britain was able to resist, but not defeat a dominant European power. In that situation Britain looked for a strong European ally (a 'continental sword') while continuing to maintain its naval power and overseas links and interests until it could once more put its own army on the continent. For this reason the period from May 1940 to June 1941 assumes a crucial importance. Having lost one 'continental sword' with the defeat of France, Britain did not stand alone, for there was still the important support of the self-governing dominions and the asset of the empire. But Britain was still without continental allies until Germany's attack on the Soviet Union brought that significant military power into the war. It is this stage of World War 2 which, above all, remains a source of enduring British pride. Germany may eventually have been defeated by a combination of the labour power of the Soviet Union in eastern Europe and US economic and military strength brought to bear in western Europe but, if Britain had been defeated in 1940 or 1941, these latter stages of the war might never have taken place.

Before this 'defining moment' came anti-climax and then defeat in Europe. The term the 'phoney war' sums up the anti-climax which many, who had been prepared for waves of bombers or great battles, felt during the first months of the war.

There was, of course, nothing phoney about the opening stages of the war from the viewpoint of the Poles. They were crushed, despite a brave defence, by the Germans and the Soviets. Britain and France could do little to help them.

There ensued a six-month period in which not a great deal happened. The French and British posture was defensive and the German generals were cautious. British civilians braced themselves for the massive air attacks that did not come; city children were evacuated to the countryside and then many drifted back to the towns; and sporting events and public entertainments were cancelled and then resumed. There was an unnatural calm before the storm.

Then came Hitler's successful war in the west. Denmark was overrun, Norway conquered, Holland, Belgium and then France surrendered and British forces were evacuated from Dunkirk. We were into the 'darkest hour'. In the event the answer was defiance: the Battle of Britain was won, the Blitz endured and there was no invasion.

The defeats in Europe in the spring of 1940 had an immediate impact upon British politics. Opinion polls, though then in their infancy, had shown Chamberlain as popular as ever in November 1939 and he commanded a substantial majority in Parliament, but by April 1940 there was widespread loss of confidence in his ability as a war leader. The failure of the Norwegian campaign resulted in a vote of no confidence in the House of Commons: the government won but some

Conservatives voted against the government and others abstained. On 10 May, Chamberlain resigned as premier and was succeeded by Winston Churchill.

The change of leadership may have improved morale but it did not change the desperate nature of the situation nor resolve the essential quandary as to what Britain should do next. The unspoken question, too delicate to be aired in public, was whether negotiations with Germany should be considered.

ACTIVITY

Write a brief answer to the following question (taking only about 15 minutes):

Should British governments have contemplated an agreement with Germany in 1940?

COMMENT

The answer must be a qualified yes. No responsible government could have totally ignored that option. In fact it was considered. You may well have answered that negotiations with Germany should have been considered and then gone on to argue that:

(a) after considering the option, it should have been immediately rejected;

(b) that after finding out what Germany's peace terms were likely to be it should have been then rejected or negotiations pursued; or

(c) that a negotiated peace was the best course in the circumstances.

That the answer was in the negative was due in large part to Winston Churchill. Was his answer correct? That it was magnificent is beyond doubt, but it is only with hindsight that it was correct. Churchill's position was insecure for he was faced with considerable opposition from the bulk of the Conservative Party. He had within his cabinet Chamberlain, Lord Halifax and R.A. Butler who were convinced that a simple refusal to contemplate a settlement was not in Britain's interest and would only prolong the war needlessly. They were not in favour of a humiliating settlement but felt that Hitler's terms should be investigated. Outside the government was the great leader of the First World War, Lloyd George, who had refused to join the government, believing that Britain's prospects were hopeless.

Though probably resolutely opposed to negotiations with Germany, Churchill did not rule them out altogether. He felt that Britain would be in a stronger position if it demonstrated that it could hold out and was able to repel any attempted German invasion. Certainly, Britain was to be in a stronger position for negotiations by the end of 1940 after the Battle of Britain; so was Churchill.

There remained, nevertheless, a case for the view held by Halifax and to some extent by Chamberlain. Britain proved in 1940 that it could hold out but its options were limited. Churchill's position was based upon faith in the British people, a belief that the Soviet-German understanding could not continue and that the USA, his literal mother country (for his mother was American), would eventually come in on the British side. Churchill's mood of defiance, his faith in the ability of the British people to continue the fight alone, and his belief that the USA would eventually join the war, are all expressed in his 'finest hour' speech. This famous oration was delivered first to the House of Commons on the afternoon of 18 June 1940 and was repeated that evening by Churchill in a radio broadcast.

ACTIVITY

Listen now to Item 6, the conclusion to Churchill's 'finest hour' speech, on your DVD.

How significant do you think this speech was for Britain in June 1940?

COMMENT

Speeches do not win wars, of course. It seems reasonable to suggest that the main significance of Churchill's oration was its propaganda value: even today the words are stirring, and, coming shortly after the evacuation from Dunkirk and the fall of France, their impact would have been all the greater. That said, however, there is a wider political significance to the speech, perhaps. Here was Churchill making a public declaration – first to Parliament, then to the nation – that Britain would continue the fight alone. By making such a public declaration, Churchill had politically out-manoeuvred those in his own Cabinet who wanted to explore the possibility of a negotiated settlement with Germany. There could now be no question of making peace with Germany as long as Churchill remained Prime Minister – and in the summer of 1940 there were no serious challengers to his position.

On the DVD (Item 7), we discuss the three leaders of Britain during the war, Chamberlain, Churchill and King George VI – two politicians and the monarch. The King symbolised and personalised the nation, while Chamberlain and Churchill provide contrasting images of leadership in war. We suggest that the contrast is not just the result of tone and style, though this is marked, but of context. Chamberlain's popularity had rested upon his relentless search for peace while Churchill's rested upon his defiant bellicosity.

ACTIVITY

Listen now to Item 7, 'Leaders', on your DVD.

Churchill's faith in the eventual outcome of the war was justified. Britain did resist the German onslaught in 1940. The following year the Soviet Union was attacked by Germany and therefore provided

Britain with the 'continental sword' that France had failed to provide. The Japanese attacked Pearl Harbor and Hitler's declaration of war on the USA brought an economic giant into the conflict. Neither development seemed likely in the early summer of 1940.

The real test of Britain came between June 1940 and June 1941: then Britain and the British Empire stood alone.

Many historians have pointed to May 1940 as marking a sea-change in British politics and opinion. Chamberlain and other proponents of appeasement were, it is held, discredited. Their policies had failed to prevent war and their prosecution of the war had been inadequate. Now there came a coalition government, headed by the leading anti-appeaser, Churchill, a man with a zest for the effective prosecution of the war, and including Labour ministers (see Figure 2).

Figure 2 *All Behind You Winston*, 14 May, 1940 (*Source*: Low, *Europe at War: A History in Sixty Cartoons with a Narrative Text*, Harmondsworth, Allen Lane, Penguin Books, 1941, p.55)

Churchill was assisted in persuading the Cabinet not to open talks with Germany by the successful evacuation of the greater part of the British Expeditionary Force from Dunkirk, albeit without most of its equipment. Dunkirk was a defeat which, by brilliant propaganda, enabled the evacuation and its means (all those little ships and boats) to appear almost a victory, and certainly a morale booster. The mythologisation of Dunkirk, and of the little ships in particular, was a process put in train concurrently with the event itself, not least in a radio broadcast by J.B. Priestley. On 5 June 1940 Priestley made the first of what was to become a regular series of 'Postscripts', talks on points of topical interest broadcast on evenings after the 9 o'clock news. We have included Priestley's broadcast on your DVD.

ACTIVITY

Listen now to Item 8, 'The epic of Dunkirk', on your DVD.

COMMENT

We haven't set a specific activity on this occasion, though you may like to consider the way in which Priestley makes the evacuation sound like a victory. And – returning to our theme of a people's war – note how he singles out in particular not just the role of the Royal Navy, but the part played in the evacuation by civilian boats.

Dunkirk was really the first occasion during the war when the boundaries between servicemen and civilians were blurred. It would not be the last.

28

The threat to Britain

Churchill exuded defiance and a determination to consider victory even while warding off defeat. The prospects did not look good. First there was the negative aim, not losing. For nearly a year after June 1940 Britain was the main object of Germany's attention. With the defeat of France, Hitler clearly believed that Britain was defeated and a peace agreement could be reached. Because of this, German preparations for 'Operation Sea Lion', the invasion of Britain, were half-hearted and were not begun until late July. Such an invasion would have been a formidable undertaking. The English Channel may be only 21 miles wide at its narrowest point, but with its relatively shallow waters, easily stirred into rough seas by strong winds, it represents a major obstacle for any invader. Germany needed command of the sea and air before any invasion stood a chance of success. The only alternative was to force a surrender by a combination of terror bombing and by sinking the ships that brought Britain its supplies.

Three campaigns were launched.

The Battle of Britain, mid-July to late October 1940
The attempt by the *Luftwaffe* to subdue the RAF and primarily its Fighter Command, which is known as the Battle of Britain, lasted from mid-July 1940 until late October. The battle was won by the fighter pilots of the RAF and by the ground staff who serviced the fighters and plotted German aircraft. Plotting German aircraft was possible because of an excellent early warning system in which radar played a key role. Factories producing aircraft also played a major role in the victory, for between 1939 and 1940 Britain increased production by 80 per cent. The main problem in the summer of 1940 was the shortage of pilots after the heavy casualties of the war in Belgium and France. Pilots from Australia, New Zealand, South Africa, Canada and Rhodesia were important in providing replacements for this initial shortage and then for the casualties of the battle over southern England. Numbers were further supplemented by pilots from the USA and from occupied European countries; there were two Polish and two Czechoslovakian squadrons. By September the *Luftwaffe* was suffering heavy losses and Hitler, enraged by the British bombing raid on Berlin in late August, ordered it to concentrate on London rather than airfields or aircraft factories.

The Blitz, September 1940 to May 1941
Then came the 'Blitz', German night-time bombing raids on British cities intended to destroy civilian morale, which lasted from September 1940 until May 1941. The attack on Coventry during the night of the

14–15 November was perhaps the single most horrifying example of what night bombing could to a medium-sized city. But it was London which experienced the most sustained attack with 200 German planes coming over London for a consecutive 57 days at the height of the Blitz. This was far from the end of aerial attacks for there were successive operations throughout the war including the Baedeker Raids, the V1 flying bombs and V2 rocket attacks, but it was the Blitz which resulted in by far the greatest destruction and the highest casualties.

The Battle of the Atlantic, from 1940
The third campaign was the attempt begun in late 1940 to deprive Britain of the food and supplies it needed to import in order to continue the war by means of sinking British ships (see *The Second World War,* pp. 135–7). The Battle of the Atlantic was as important as the Battle of Britain. By June 1941 German U-boats had sunk 5.7 million tons of Allied shipping. Although still neutral, the USA began escorting convoys between its territorial waters and Iceland in May 1941 and the Royal Canadian Navy, tiny at the beginning of the war, expanded rapidly and played a significant role in the struggle to maintain Britain's supplies. The success of the U-boats was such that they seemed to have the upper hand for more than a year after US entry into the war. The Battle of the Atlantic was almost certainly a more close-run struggle than the Battle of Britain. It was to continue until nearly the end of the war but to have further intensified attacks on shipping in the first half of 1941 probably represented Germany's best chance of knocking Britain out of the war.

Of these three campaigns, the first was fought between servicemen, the third between the U-boats of the German Navy and the Royal Navy together with the British Merchant Navy, while the second saw British civilians on the front line.

What if the Germans had invaded Britain?

Britain was *not* invaded. Just as Napoleon's armies had massed on the shores of the Channel and been frustrated by the Channel itself, by the weather and by the Royal Navy, so, with the addition of the RAF, were Hitler's: 'Operation Sea Lion' was postponed at the end of 1940.

Had a landing been successful, a sufficient beach-head been established and Panzer and mechanised infantry divisions allowed to group, it is very possible, perhaps probable, that, with the British army still in disarray after Dunkirk, Britain would have been defeated. No doubt King and government would have been evacuated, probably to Canada, to continue resistance from there, but what would Britain under the swastika have been like? With the experience of occupied Europe to go on, it is tempting to indulge in 'counter-factual' history.

There is little doubt that the degree of resistance in German-occupied Europe, especially between 1940 and 1943, has been much exaggerated. There were of course many examples of heroic defiance and there were underground organisations but, after initial despair and bewilderment, life went on. The police were back on the streets of Belgium, of occupied France and of the other countries under direct or indirect German rule; bread was baked and people went to work as usual. Post-war France found it very difficult to come to terms with the history of occupied France and that of the greater part of France (governed from Vichy) that was not occupied until 1943.

Would Britain have been different? Would there have been fighting not just on the beaches but in the hills, the countryside and the towns, or would there have been widespread collaboration with the new order? Collaboration might not necessarily have been only the active collaboration of those prepared to take office (whether in Whitehall or town hall), but also the passive collaboration of those who felt they had little choice but to cooperate if they were to earn a living and feed their children.

We can only pose the question. The British of 1940 were a proud, a homogeneous and a patriotic people but the pressures would have been considerable. As it happens one part of the British Isles was occupied. The Channel Islands were, understandably, not considered defensible and were occupied from 1940 until the end of the war. However, the geography and the modest population of the islands militate against drawing much in the way of conclusions about an imaginary occupation of Britain.

Yet if Britain never experienced the reality of invasion, the threat of invasion was very real, especially in the summer of 1940. This threat presented the government's propagandists with something of a dilemma. On the one hand there was a need to instruct people what to do in the event of an invasion. On the other hand, however, there was a need to reassure people that, if an invasion came, it would be dealt with by the army. Churchill suggested the slogan 'You can always take one with you', suggesting that people should fight and be prepared to die, though this idea was rejected on the grounds that it was too defeatist. Instead, all households were sent a leaflet entitled 'If the Invader Comes', which included commonsense and practical instructions, such as locking away maps and disabling motor vehicles. There was also a short instructional film entitled *Miss Grant Goes to the Door*, made by the Ministry of Information (MOI), in the summer of 1940. This film was not very well regarded, largely because it was a fictional story about two elderly ladies who find a dead parachutist in their garden and then unmask a German spy, disguised as a British officer, when he makes silly mistakes such as asking for directions to 'Yarvis Cross' rather than 'Jarvis Cross'. Fortunately the two ladies have armed themselves with a revolver which the dead parachutist had conveniently tucked in his boot! This was hardly a very likely scenario, as an article in the film journal *Documentary News Letter* made clear:

> A film on how to deal with a parachutist has drawn wide public comment – as any cinema-goer with ears will notice – because it provides the person meeting the German parachutist with a revolver taken from a dead German; most of us have no revolvers and not all of us can expect to find a dead German available.

> (*Documentary News Letter*, September 1940, p.6)

The script writer Rodney Ackland later revealed that the version of the film released to cinemas had been a re-shoot because the original was deemed too frightening to show to the public.

Although most historians would now probably agree that the likelihood of a German invasion had passed by September 1940, and that Hitler's invasion of the Soviet Union made an invasion of Britain even less likely thereafter, there were still occasional invasion scares in Britain during 1941 and 1942. Early in 1942, following a series of military reverses – including the fall of Singapore and the 'Channel dash' of the German battle cruisers *Scharnhorst* and *Gneisenau* – there was renewed anxiety in Britain and a series of scares, albeit largely exaggerated by the press.

It was in order to guard against complacency that the film production company Ealing Studios, in cooperation with the MOI and the War Office, made a fictional feature film called *Went the Day Well?* (1942). Derived from a magazine story by Graham Greene, *Went the Day Well?* (Greene, 1999) was a dramatic story in which a party of Royal Engineers who arrive in a quiet English village turn out to be the advance guard of a German invasion force. It also suggested, controversially, that the local squire, a respected pillar of the community, was in fact a German agent, thus tapping into the fears about fifth columnists and quislings that had haunted British minds since the fall of Norway in 1940. The film showed the villagers fighting back against the invaders, and, unlike the rather farcical *Miss Grant Goes to the Door*, did so with a degree of realism and brutality that was unusual for a film of the time. Although the invaders are defeated in the end, many of the villagers are killed, and in this respect the film recalls Churchill's aborted slogan, 'You can always take one

34

Yet again the summer of 1940 has been identified as the crucial moment when attitudes began to change. As the historian Paul Addison commented in his book *The Road to 1945*:

> The year 1940 has gone down in our annals as the time when all sections of the nation put aside their peacetime differences, and closed ranks under the leadership of Churchill – 'their finest hour'. It should also go down as the year when the foundations of political power shifted decisively leftward for a decade.

(Addison, 1975, p.17)

It was in the aftermath of Dunkirk, in particular, that discussion about post-war reconstruction began to feature prominently in the media: in the letters columns of newspapers, in radio talks and even in official films. Commentators, especially on the left, argued that as the war had brought about full employment (or at least something very close to it), then it should be possible to maintain this once the war was over. After the war, it was believed, there would be an overwhelming need for reconstruction: not just the physical reconstruction of buildings that had been destroyed, but the social reconstruction of a more just and egalitarian society in which the demons of unemployment, poverty and social deprivation would be banished.

On the DVD we discuss the extent to which the population was inspired by a vision of a new, changed Britain, or was happy enough to work and fight for the Britain that it knew.

ACTIVITY

Now listen to Item 9, 'People', on your DVD.

Looking at the sort of discussion and debate that took place about the future of British society after the war, we include a short official film called *The Dawn Guard* that was released early in 1941. It was made for the Ministry of Information (MOI) by John and Roy Boulting, twin brothers who were known for their 'progressive' social and political views.

Now watch Item 10, '*The Dawn Guard*', on your DVD.

Then jot down a short answer to each of the following questions:

1 What is the theme of the film?

2 Would you say that this source represents a particular political ideology?

COMMENT

1 In the film, two men – the older man conservative and backward-looking, the younger man progressive and forward-looking – present 'two ways of looking at this war'. One view (the one 'we are officially encouraged to adopt' according to a broadcast by J.B. Priestley at the time) is to see war aims simply in terms of defeating fascism. Priestley talked of Hitler and Mussolini as a 'terrible interruption', and the old man in the film complains of the Nazis 'upsetting the ways and wrecking the lives of millions of people'. This view ('to get our lives back to where they was') is contrasted with the notion that people saw the war as an opportunity to achieve social justice. The aim here is to

All, or at least many, of the restrictions placed upon individual liberty can be justified in the circumstances, but the direct and indirect control of the media does make it difficult to assess public opinion. The Ministry of Information had considerable power but most of the censorship in the media was self-censorship done at source. Government controlled the news in the interests of the war effort and it also controlled, or limited, comment. The main political parties were united in their support for the war but especially in the first two years of the war there was opposition or questioning from the extreme right and left.

The British Union of Fascists was obviously under suspicion, despite Sir Oswald Mosley's professions of patriotism; after all the security services knew full well that the party had received financial support from Italy and Germany. Communists and 'fellow-travellers' were also critical of the war and enjoyed financial support from the Soviet Union but changed their line in June 1941 when Hitler invaded the Soviet Union. The *Daily Worker* – official mouthpiece of the Communist Party of Great Britain – was closed by order of the Home Secretary when it argued the official Communist line (before Hitler's invasion of the Soviet Union) that the war was a war between capitalist states and should not be supported. The *Daily Mirror*, however, which supported the war effort but criticised the government's conduct of it, escaped with a stern warning.

Between these extremes, in 1939 there was a substantial body of opinion which believed that the declaration of war on Germany was a mistake. Many who thought this changed their view once Britain was at war, but there were many others who, while entirely patriotic and committed to the war effort, were apprehensive not just about the prospects of victory but about the effects of the strains of war on the British economy and Britain's position in the world. The view that the Soviet Union presented a greater threat to British interests than a Germany that was likely to be content to enjoy a domination of the continent and allow Britain to concentrate upon the Empire had some support in influential circles.

Recent wars, the Falkland or the Gulf Wars, have been far enough removed from the national survival of Britain for the media to continue largely unimpeded. World War 2 was different. Just as it is impossible to imagine a retired general being interviewed on radio in 1942 and being asked by a presenter 'Now, how do you think General Montgomery will plan to deal with General Rommel's threat to Egypt?', so no dissenting voices were to be heard on the practicality of fighting on after Dunkirk.

Britain in 1940 was a tightly controlled society and continued to be so during the following years; less tightly controlled politically than Germany or the Soviet Union, but in terms of life-style, limitations on movement and choice for consumers, probably more constricted than Germany before 1943.

Now read Chapter 4 of *The Second World War*. This will provide information about the way other combatant powers as well as Britain controlled their war efforts and maintained morale.

Some historians have argued that the economic policies adopted by the government to direct the war effort – including conscription, rationing, fixed prices and the direction of labour – gave rise to a phenomenon known as 'War Socialism'. A.J.P. Taylor, for example, wrote that:

> … in the end direction and control turned Great Britain into a country more fully socialist than anything ever achieved by the conscious planners of Soviet Russia.

(English History 1914–1945, 1965, p.507)

The important point to recognise here, however, is that as far as Churchill and the Conservative Party were concerned, this was a temporary expedient necessary for the efficient conduct of the war effort. The Labour Party and their supporters, however, saw increased levels of state control over industry and the economy as the way forward. The setting up of the modern Welfare State and the nationalisation of key industries under the post-war Labour government was to a large extent derived from the wartime example.

The effects of rationing

Rationing was introduced for petrol in September 1939, for food in January 1940 and was eventually extended to clothes. What food was rationed and how much you were able to buy of a particular foodstuff with your ration card varied at different stages of the war but most with the exception of bread and potatoes were eventually rationed.

How willingly did the population go along with this? Does the evidence point to a patriotic and responsible people or to a populace determined to find a way round the rules and to get what they wanted on the 'black market'?

Much has been made of the virtues of the wartime diet and it was undoubtedly sufficient to keep people healthy if adhered to though probably inadequate for those engaged in heavy manual work. It was, however, boring and somewhat stodgy.

The diary of Miss Vere Hodgson, a social worker in Holland Park, London, for the second half of 1941 gives a glimpse of the hardships:

> 18 July. I was heavily told off by the Kensington Salvage Council for throwing away a crust of mouldy bread and therefore wasting food [the bread should have been set aside for the salvage collectors and used to feed pigs].
>
> 28 November. My first egg for a fortnight turned out to be bad … Tea scarce, no milk to put in it.
>
> 9 December. Pears have been seen in some shops, I hear, but at three shillings each.
>
> (Quoted in Leonard Mosely, *Backs to the Wall,* 1971, pp.232–3)

The 'black market' is a wide term and taken strictly it includes organised operations as well as the regular customer (such as Corporal and butcher Jones of the TV series *Dad's Army*) getting a few extra sausages; or the town-dweller with rural relations going home with some bacon and eggs after a visit to the farm. (Though a comedy series, *Dad's Army* brilliantly resurrected central war-time stereotypes including the decent but pompous patriot, the 'spiv' and the 'little Hitler', as those, like the ARP commander, who enjoyed their temporary power to boss people around were called.) The red petrol allocated to farms was frequently misused: a pig in the back of the pick-up could justify a drive to the pub. West-End restaurants were not allowed to charge more than 5 shillings for a meal but could include a cover charge. Gossip columnist and MP 'Chips' Channon wrote in his diary on 5 November 1940, after he and friends had consumed five magnums of champagne at the Dorchester:

> London lives well: I've never seen more lavishness, more money spent, or more food consumed than tonight, and the dance floor was packed.

One problem was the differing experiences of town and countryside. It would have been optimistic to expect the producers of food to limit their own consumption to what government considered the requisite amount, or, indeed, to have denied friends and neighbours a little extra. In any case, rural areas had a greater ability to expand food supplies that were not rationed. A compilation of recollections from the Sussex village of Steyning reveals the way that people kept hens and expanded vegetable plots, while rabbits supplemented the food that was on ration (Ian Ivatt, *Food for Thought: Wartime in Steyning*, 2000). As Stanley

Jones who grew up in wartime Trowbridge recollects, he came home from school at lunchtime to

> … a good dinner of rabbit stew – with always plenty of home-grown vegetables from my father's allotment. There was still some meat (apparently not rationed) such as pigs' heads, trotters, tails, hearts, liver etc., which mum would make up into tasty meals …
>
> (BBC *WW2 People's War*, Stanley Jones)

The police stopped cars returning from the increasingly rare Sunday trips to the countryside and searched the under-carriages for bacon and hams.

Clearly the response to rationing, shortages and government exhortations to limit unnecessary consumption varied widely. Some were, no doubt, scrupulous in consuming only what they were officially allowed. The royal family were almost ostentatious in their austerity and Windsor and Buckingham Palace became notorious for their unheated rooms, shallow baths and frugal fare – 'Spam on a gold plate' as A.J.P. Taylor has described it. Eleanor Roosevelt was astonished at the discomfort. Queen Elizabeth on a visit to a northern town commented on the lavish lunch at the town hall, protesting that they never had anything like this at home. 'Ah well then, thou'll be glad of a bit of a do like this' answered the mayor (Theo Aronson, *The Royal Family at War,* 1993, pp. 114–5).

The government certainly took the need for rationing seriously, hectoring the population to avoid illicit supplies and suggesting imaginative recipes that did not involve eggs, meat or sugar. Lord Woolton, Minister for Food, gave his name to the infamous Woolton Pie and tried in vain to get the population to delight in whale meat. There was even a *Kitchen Front* series on the radio.

ACTIVITY

Can we really assess the impact of rationing, the degree to which it was accepted and the degree to which people got round it?

Write a brief answer (spend only about 10 minutes on this activity).

COMMENT

You probably answered that we can agree on a broad picture of a reduction in living standards, a more basic diet and difficulties in obtaining luxuries but that the degree to which it was possible to supplement rations and evade the restrictions must have varied widely. By its very nature, it is almost impossible to assess the extent of the black market. You may have wondered how much we can rely on oral history here. Such evidence is undoubtedly illuminating when it comes to how families made do with their meagre rations and legally supplemented them, but do many people really tell the truth, even long after the event when it comes to the ways round the regulations? Few will say 'Oh yes, Dad made a fortune on the black market and we lived like kings'.

Shortages were just as much a problem as rationing. Cigarettes and beer were not rationed but were in short supply. You had to be a good friend of the publican or have a good scouting system which discovered which pub had beer that day to get your normal quota. If the usual cigarettes were not available you could usually get an obnoxious brand, Pasha, from Turkey, though the more ingenious took to growing their own tobacco or scouring hedgerows for herbal substitutes. On the whole, however, the government recognised that tobacco, like tea, was necessary for the war effort.

The impact of the Blitz and other bombing raids on morale

What impact did the Blitz of 1940 and later bombing raids have on morale? One problem we are faced with here is censorship. Obviously a newspaper headline reading 'Bombing raids cause mass panic and calls for peace at any price' wouldn't have been allowed. But there were, not surprisingly, occasions on which there were something close to mass panics, instances where those in authority deserted their posts and there were great exoduses from towns to surrounding fields:

> A report on Coventry [by the Ministry of Information], for example, referred to 'great depression, a widespread feeling of impotence and many open signs of hysteria'. In Portsmouth a report stated 'that looting and wanton destruction had reached alarming proportions. The police seem unable to exercise control.
>
> (M. Donnelly, *Britain and the Second World War*, 1999, p.37)

Yet the overwhelming impression that historians have come to is that panic was rare and that there was more insouciance and defiance than fear. People were determined to and contrived to get on with as normal a life as was possible. Upper-class social life had an air of determined hedonism: there were parties, the gentlemen's clubs remained open as did the best hotels and restaurants even when the one next door had just been bombed. Equally in the London docklands, the pubs remained open, provided there was beer, and cinemas were crowded. There was some bravado about this: people may have acted out parts and repeated phrases learned from others or from the radio to conceal sorrow and fear, but that's probably what communal bravery is about.

The way that morale survived is remarkable indeed when you consider that

> … from the opening of the Night Blitz on 7 September 1940 to the end of that year, 22,069 civilians were killed in the British Isles, 13,390 of them in London.
>
> (John Ray, *The Night Blitz,* 1996, p.260)

A respondent to the BBC's *WW2 People's War* website recounts once joining the crowds who sheltered in the tube stations:

> I'll never forget it. Everybody shared space and food and once the younger children were settled down, the adults had a singsong, or played cards. With all those people packed along the platform, the air left something to be desired; despite the discomforts, there was no denying the friendly atmosphere, but I never repeated the experience.
>
> (BBC *WW2 People's War*, Dobbie Dobinson)

That the experience was never repeated is significant. The communal nature of sheltering from the bombing has been much exaggerated. Sheltering in tube stations or public shelters presented a picture attractive to journalists, but most people took shelter under their own stairs or in the Anderson shelters, corrugated iron constructions, buried in their gardens.

If London endured the most sustained bombing raids, the massive and effective raid on Coventry is well known, while every dockyard town, naval port, manufacturing area or railway nexus got its share. A Mass-Observation observer in Newcastle reported:

> Women are particularly sick of these raids. I've talked to dozens and they all affirm this war is very much worse than the last and they are *sick to death of it.*
>
> (Dorothy Sheridan (ed.), *Wartime Women: A Mass-Observation Anthology*, 1990, p.118)

There were instances of panic, hysteria and looting during and after air raids, and of resentment by those in areas that were heavily bombed against those in more fortunate neighbourhoods. This could take the form of class-based resentment or of animosity between town and country: '*They* don't get bombed and live well; *we* have to take in their evacuees.'

If a story of uniform cheerfulness and defiance will not stand up, the overwhelming evidence is that resilience and patriotism were very evident. They were also evident in Germany during the later stages of the war. Bombing provoked as much anger and defiance as fear.

Now we'd like you to look at two sources that depict the effects of the Blitz on London. The first is a radio report by Ed Murrow, an American broadcaster, from the steps of St Martin-in-the-Fields on 24 August 1940. The second source is a short documentary film entitled *London Can Take It!*, made for the Ministry of Information by the GPO Film Unit and released in October 1940. *London Can Take It!* was introduced and narrated by another US journalist, Quentin Reynolds, who was the London correspondent of the magazine *Collier's Weekly*. The film was made in the first place for export to the USA, but it was also shown in British cinemas, albeit with a different title, *Britain Can Take It!*, to recognise that other cities besides London had been on the receiving end of aerial bombing.

ACTIVITY

Listen to Item 11, 'Trafalgar Square', on your DVD.

Then watch Item 12, '*London Can Take It!*'

After listening to and viewing these items, write a short answer to each of the following questions (this should take about 30 minutes):

1 How would you compare the value of the two items as historical sources?

2 What do you think is the significance of using American commentators on both these items?

3 What was the propaganda objective of *London Can Take It!*?

COMMENT

1   The principal value of the Murrow broadcast is its immediacy: it provides an eye-witness account of air-raid precautions broadcast as the warning sirens are sounded. *London Can Take It!* is less immediate, as the film material has been selected and edited, and a commentary written and recorded. That said, however, it is still close to the events and provides us with visual evidence of the London Blitz.

2   The Americans provide a supposedly 'neutral' perspective on events (note especially Reynolds's assertion towards the end of the commentary to *London Can Take It!*: 'I am a neutral reporter'). This would have the effect, or so it was hoped, of making the reports seem less like official propaganda and more like news items. This was particularly important for overseas audiences, especially in the still-neutral USA (remember that *London Can Take It!* was initially intended for US audiences).

3   London Can Take It! is clearly intended to assert the resilience of Londoners to the Blitz: note how the commentary repeatedly stresses that the bombing, far from weakening people's will to fight, does precisely the opposite and strengthens their determination. It also emphasises national unity and social cohesion amongst 'the people of Churchill's Island'. It promotes the notion of the people's war with its references to 'the people's army of volunteers'. The film does not conceal the damage that is being done, and it does acknowledge that people are being killed in the nightly raids, though it does not dwell on the losses and there are no shots of casualties. There is also a reference to British bombing raids on Germany, assuring audiences that Britain is not only 'taking it', but dishing it out too.

London Can Take It! was widely distributed – the British version of the film was shown on all cinema programmes by an agreement between the MOI and the cinema exhibitors – and there is much evidence to suggest that it was well received. Basil Wright, a left-wing film critic writing for the right-wing *Spectator*, was particularly approving of the theme of the people's war:

> And in all truth this message about our civilian army dominates the film ... For this is a film of the people who, in the end and on their own terms, will win the war for freedom and democracy ... It is the first film clearly to state this important fact. In its pellucid and brilliant camerawork, its leisurely and emphatic cutting and its economy of emphasis, it clears the whole air of dunderhead and paralysing verbiage about the war. It states facts, but with the addition of true drama and true poetry.

(*Spectator*, 25 October 1940, p.415)

It was not only film critics who approved. Mass-Observation reported that, amongst their respondents, it was 'the most frequently commented on film, and received nothing but praise'. And when it was shown as part of a non-theatrical film show in a Scottish mining village early in 1941, the projectionist reported:

> *Britain Can Take It!* was by far the most successful film. The reasons, I think, were because of the neutral reporter, the emphasis on the common people and the fact that it showed what the war was like.
>
> (*Documentary News Letter*, July 1941, p.129)

The image of the British people stoically carrying on under enemy bombardment has become one of the enduring myths of the war. We use the word 'myths' not to imply that this image is incorrect, but rather that it accords with the widely held popular view of the war. We can compare *London Can Take It!* with other accounts of the fortitude of British people under fire. Here, for example, is an extract from a letter from the film-maker Humphrey Jennings to his wife in 1940:

> Some of the damage in London is pretty heart-breaking, but what an effect it has had on the people! What warmth – what courage! What determination! People sternly encouraging each other by explaining that when you hear a bomb whistle it means it has missed you! People in the north singing in public shelters: 'One man went to mow – went to mow a meadow'. [Women's Voluntary Services] WVS [...] girls serving hot drinks to firefighters during air raids explaining that really they were 'terribly afraid all the time'! ... Everybody absolutely determined: secretly delighted with the *privilege* of holding up Hitler. Certain of beating him: a certainty which no amount of bombing can weaken, only strengthen ... Maybe by the time you get this one or two more 18th cent[ury] churches will be smashed up in London: some civilians killed: some personal loves and treasures wrecked – but it means nothing; a curious kind of unselfishness is developing which can stand all that and more. We have found ourselves on the right side and on the right track at last!
>
> (Mary-Lou Jennings (ed.), *Humphrey Jennings: Film-maker, Painter, Poet*, 1982, p.23)

As a private letter, rather than something written for public consumption, we have no reason to doubt the sincerity of Jennings's account of the Blitz. Three years later Jennings himself made his own contribution to what historian Angus Calder later called 'the myth of the Blitz'. Jennings's film *Fires Were Started* (1943), made for the

Crown Film Unit (as the GPO Film Unit had become), was a sincere and moving tribute to the role of the Auxiliary Fire Service during the winter of 1940–41. Jennings himself was a keen social observer – he had been involved in the foundation of Mass-Observation in 1937 – and, like so many middle-class intellectuals, was passionately interested in the lives of 'ordinary' people. He spent months living and researching with real auxiliary firemen and based the characters in his film on real people, casting real firemen rather than actors.

Interestingly, *Fires Were Started* contains two scenes that would seem to have been inspired by Jennings's letter to his wife: a scene where the firemen sing 'One man went to mow' while preparing for their night's work, and another where a mobile canteen staffed by WVS women serves them tea after they have extinguished a fire.

Popular support for the war effort

Did people support and believe in the policies of the government and its assurances about the course of the war? There is evidence of a spirit of defiance in the face of the Blitz, but there's also the rather awkward evidence that, having listened to the BBC News, more than half of the population tuned into the propagandist voice of Germany, William Joyce, 'Lord Haw-Haw'. His acquired English upper-class accent only just concealing his Irish intonations, Joyce broadcast nightly to the British public with his accounts and tales of British setbacks and his view of the war as opposed to that of the ordinary British people and achieved a considerable audience. Why did people tune in to him and how seriously did they take his broadcasts? Most claimed to listen to him 'for a laugh' but there was also a suspicion that the BBC News was doctored, and, to an extent, it was.

A respondent to the BBC's *WW2 People's War* recounts her mother-in-law's experience of the war in Plymouth, which as a major naval base was frequently bombed:

> During Lord Haw Haw's broadcasts he would say he knew that the people of Plymouth were going up to the moors and that the bombs would get them as well, that there was no hiding place from Germany.

> Although I have read that he was considered a laughing stock, my mother-in-law was quite scared of his broadcasts. She said he seemed to have a knowledge of local places and knew what people were doing and when. She said his broadcasts were so accurate about the activities and movements of the people of Plymouth it made her feel he was right there among them.

> (BBC *WW2 People's War*, Pat Hughes)

A basic patriotism and a scepticism about the truth of government pronouncements are not incompatible.

Can we talk of a people united behind the war effort?

Well, we would be naïve to expect to find evidence of perfection. In almost every society and situation people will be torn between self-interest, however short-term, and the public interest. There are, nevertheless, some awkward questions. Should we expect to find strikes in war-time Britain, profiteers or a high crime rate?

The much vaunted effects of wartime controls and planning resulted in low productivity per worker. There was a rigid adherence to craft demarcations and over-manning in the shipyards and other industries. It has been argued (see Corelli Barnett, *The Audit of War,* 1986) that far from a 'people's war' with everyone working for a common cause, the figures for strikes and absenteeism during the war reveal a home front in which the trade unions and workforce simply took advantage of wartime full-employment. If a free-market economy is far from immune to corruption, a command economy, in which orders are placed by officials, can be worse, and there was great suspicion of the newly rich hauliers and suppliers. It must have been difficult for the crew of a ship that had made its way across a U-boat-riddled sea to find that the dockers were on strike and that one couldn't get home because the railway workers were also on strike.

Crime rates are always difficult to assess. Government regulations such as rationing invented new crimes. In London the black market provided opportunities for criminals and deserters from the armed forces who drifted into the city. The blackout made their work easier. Petty dishonesty seems to have increased, such as taking goods from work and buying forged ration cards. There was also a modest increase in the murder rate, a bigger increase in the number of violent crimes and a sharp increase in the incidence of rape.

Did the people come together?

The usual depiction of war-time Britain is of a coming together of classes and of town and country. The experience of the evacuation of children from town to the safer country is often said to have introduced one world to another. The first wave departed in September 1939 – London children being seen off by the Labour leader of the London County Council, Herbert Morrison, with the words 'Keep a cheerful British smile on your face ... Good luck, and a safe return to dear old London'.

By May 1940, many evacuees had drifted back to the towns but there was then a further wave of evacuees. Evelyn Waugh's *Put Out More*

Flags (1942) is a wonderfully funny satire on the first wave of evacuation. Evacuation certainly introduced one Britain to another but, as is noted in *The Second World War* (p.125), whether they always liked each other is open to question. Oral evidence from evacuees reveals kindliness, hostility, incomprehension and even cruelty. Many evacuees treasured their relationships with rural foster parents and visited them for the rest of their lives; others shuddered at the memory of their transplant to a hostile environment.

One evacuee experienced both a kindly welcome and uncaring neglect. In one temporary home (in Southport) she and her brother:

> ... had to sit in the scullery to eat while they sat at a table in the living room. I can only remember eating bread and cornflakes there, never a cooked meal. We were always hungry. She was never in when we got home from school so we had to wait outside. The daughter went to an aunt after school. Often air raid sirens would start as we were waiting to get into the house and we had to run to the nearest shelter. We were very frightened.

Later she was billeted with a farming family in Herefordshire:

> I became part of their family in a way I don't think even they were aware. Their unassuming kindness was measureless. The happy memories of a town child getting to know the countryside would fill a book.

(BBC *WW2 People's War*, 'Evacuation from Bootle to Herefordshire')

The war made for a much more mobile society, despite petrol rationing, though travelling on trains crowded with troops became more difficult. People who might in peacetime have rarely left their home town or village found themselves in barracks or air bases, munitions and armaments factories, and farms scattered around Britain, while servicemen saw many parts of the world in very inhospitable circumstances. The degree to which the war encouraged greater social mobility or closer relations between different sections of society has been much debated.

This is a common theme in war-time films and radio. Clearly the war brought into close contact many people who would never have mixed in peace-time life. On the other hand, many social groups spent the war years in the company of their social peers. It may well be that often, in a uniformed society, rank became more important than class, but rank still tended to shadow class. One of Mass-Observation's female respondents who served in the WAAF wrote about competition for men.

... to get a man is not sufficient. It's easy to get a man. In fact it's difficult not to ... the desirable qualities are rank, wings, looks, money, youth in that order. Rank is unbelievably important.

(Calder and Sheridan, *Speak for Yourself*, p.133)

Another WAAF woman wrote that recruits initially broke up into cliques based on their civilian social positions but that this was modified as the week went on by three main circumstances: 'trade and social class; hut, squadron, flight; and physique'. She also considered that the reasons given for joining up had '... very little to do with "doing one's bit". General boredom with life was the keynote' (Calder and Sheridan, *Speak for Yourself*, pp.130–1).

Women and the war

Women's experience of the war is a much reiterated theme. Rightly so in one sense, for this was a war in which the unmarried female population was mobilised for the war effort, wore uniforms and, if not in the armed forces, served as land girls, nurses, or in factories. Perhaps, however, this misses the main point, which is that women, if not part of the 'sharp end' of the military, were *integrated* into the war effort.

What comes across in women's accounts of their war experiences is not any concept of a separate war but the trepidation and exhilaration they felt in becoming an essential part of a greater whole, a nation at arms. A very few women may have wished to fly fighter planes or bombers, or to have been in the front line of an infantry attack; some women flew transport aircraft; others were resourceful and brave agents in France; but very many relished finding that they had the ability or could acquire the skills that made them indispensable to the nation's ability to wage war.

Women, it could be said, provided the auxiliary capacity of the war machine, but the dependency of the front line on the auxiliary was a feature of modern warfare. The result was a modification of the relations between men and women, rather than a radical adjustment: more sexual freedom, easier social relations and a sense of comradeship. It's anachronistic to think that most women wanted to go back to a different world 'after the war was over', rather than the traditional world in which, by and large, men earned the income and women looked after the home. But after women had charted the planes of the *Luftwaffe* during the Battle of Britain; as mechanics prepared bombers and fighters for combat; wept for those who had not returned, then raised a glass in the pub to their memory, something had changed.

Of course it was not just RAF crews we mixed with … [one
WAAF recollects] … Australians, New Zealanders and Canadians
too were often stationed with us, and in between their exhausting
schedule of missions the local village pub would often echo to
their own particular songs and ribaldry. And likewise too, many of
these young men had their own lives cut cruelly short over skies so
very far from their own homes and loved ones. In fact, I well
remember it was the tradition in one local pub that each airman
had his own decorated tankard that the landlord kept hung up over
the bar. Needless to say, by the time I was posted away from the
neighbouring station there were an awful lot of tankards hanging
there that would never again grace their owners' lips with a
refreshing pint. Paradoxically, it is sometimes trivial little details
like that that bring home the true horror of war.

(BBC *WW2 People's War*, Eileen Jones)

Women, the government realised, were important to the war. Married
women and especially those with children were exempt from
conscription but had to manage to run households amidst food
shortages, carry children out to air-raid shelters, and take in evacuees
or have their own children evacuated to distant places. Unmarried
women could serve with the armed forces, join the Land Army or find
or be directed to many other essential duties including taking on roles
normally performed by men (see *The Second World War*, pp.125–6).

The feature film *Millions Like Us* (1943) illustrates the desire of the
authorities to show women's important contribution to the armed
forces, to encourage female participation and, at the same time, to
demonstrate that women of all classes could forge common bonds in
serving their country. The film was written and directed by Frank
Launder and Sidney Gilliat. This film was originally planned as a
documentary for the Ministry of Information, but as Launder and
Gilliat developed the script, they realised it would be more appropriate
as a feature film and so it was turned over to a commercial company,
Gainsborough Pictures, to produce. In the extract, the heroine, a young
unmarried woman called Celia (Patricia Roc), has been called up for
her interview at the Ministry of Labour and National Service. We have
included a short extract from this film on your DVD.

ACTIVITY

Now watch Item 13, '*Millions Like Us*', on your DVD, then answer the
following three questions:

1   What is the propaganda message of this scene?

expensive British film of the war. It was produced with the cooperation of the Ministry of Information, which arranged for location filming to be undertaken in Eire (for the spectacular staging of the Battle of Agincourt), and for Olivier to be released from his wartime service in the Fleet Air Arm.

Rural England and cathedral towns often dominated in appeals to patriotism, again represented by films such as *The Demi-Paradise* (1943) and *A Canterbury Tale* (1944). On the other hand, there were many documentary films in which the social realist school provided a gritty industrial, urban view of contemporary Britain, just as romantic in an inverted way. This was apparent not just in official documentaries such as *Wales – Green Mountain, Black Mountain* (1944), written by Dylan Thomas and focusing on the Welsh coal-mining industry, but also in feature films such as *The Shipbuilders* (1943) and *Love on the Dole* (1941). The last film, based on Walter Greenwood's depression-era novel of the Salford slums, had been blocked by the British Board of Film Censors in the 1930s but was allowed during the war because it fitted the wartime mood of optimism for a better future and because unemployment was no longer a major social problem. Somewhere between these different images of Britain were films about the suburban lower middle classes, such as *This Happy Breed* (1944). And there were frankly unusual and experimental films, such as *They Came to a City* (1944), adapted from a play by J.B. Priestley, an allegorical fantasy story about nine people who are brought to the gates of an unseen city (implicitly representing a planned welfare society) and have to decide whether they will choose to live there or not.

The most celebrated films of the war, such as Noel Coward's patriotic tribute to the Royal Navy in *In Which We Serve* (1942) and Anthony Asquith and Terence Rattigan's quietly contemplative *The Way to the Stars* (1945), about life on and around an RAF base during the war, tended to focus on the armed services. One of the most controversial films of the war – controversial to the extent that no less a figure than Churchill attempted (unsuccessfully) to ban it – was *The Life and Death of Colonel Blimp* (1943). 'Colonel Blimp' was the creation of cartoonist David Low (see Figure 3) and was used as a satirical figure to ridicule military incompetence and political reactionaries. Churchill objected to the film, written and directed by Michael Powell and Emeric Pressburger, on the grounds that 'I am not prepared to allow propaganda detrimental to the morale of the Army'. In the event he was persuaded that the government had no legal powers to prevent the film from being made and that to do so would appear a repressive and illiberal move in a democracy. However, the MOI and War Office refused to cooperate with the film-makers, for example in refusing on this occasion to facilitate Laurence Olivier's release from the services to play 'Colonel Blimp' (Roger Livesey, who was not in the services, was cast instead). The film went on to be one of the biggest box-office successes of the year, helped no doubt by the controversy: there are reports that cinemas advertised it with the slogan 'See the banned film!'

Figure 3   *Col. Blimp Under Steam*, 23 May, 1934
(*Source*: Low, *Low's Political Parade: With Colonel Blimp*, London, The Cresset Press, 1936, (n.p.))

The monarchy

If Britain's self-image of its unified and divided self at war was complex, one personification of the nation was all but unquestioned – the monarchy. King George VI, Queen Elizabeth and their daughters were, undoubtedly, enormously important to the projection of a nation at war. Do we put this down to the atavistic instinct that caused a population under extreme pressure to turn to the oldest form of leadership? Was it because the monarchy was enthusiastically supported by all major political parties and being 'above politics' was therefore the natural repository of patriotism even when there was a coalition government? Was it due to the brilliant command of public relations demonstrated by the Queen (rather better at it than Churchill or Attlee), or to sympathy for the King who, not well suited to his position, so earnestly struggled to fulfil it?

As we discuss in Item 7 on the DVD, King George VI, who, of course, had come to the throne with the abdication of his brother, Edward VIII, had a bad stammer which he struggled to overcome.

The royal family was seen as an elevated yet normal British family, subject to bombing and common hardships. The princesses Elizabeth and Margaret addressed the children of the nation on the radio and, later, Elizabeth in ATS uniform wrestled with the mechanics of an army truck. George VI made no great decisions; the mistakes and achievements were due to Churchill and his government. Yet, loyalty and patriotism were focused on the monarchy more than upon Churchill and/or Attlee.

A WIDER WAR

Between June 1940 and June 1941, Britain, with considerable support from the British Empire, proved that it could withstand the power of Germany and a German-dominated western Europe. Britain's problem was where it could take positive action against the enemy. An invasion of western Europe was out of the question, for Britain had neither the human resources nor the military hardware to mount such an invasion with any expectation of success.

ACTIVITY

Now read Chapters 3 and 5 of *The Second World War*.

The failure of the Dieppe Raid in August 1942, where Canadian troops made up 80 per cent of the landing force and out of 4963 men there were 3367 casualties, later demonstrated this only too clearly. Only two limited options were available to Britain: to launch an offensive against the Italian forces in Africa and Greece and to bomb Germany. Both were adopted.

Bomber Command's efforts were relatively ineffective during 1940 and 1941 and were costly in terms of the losses of men and aircraft but laid the foundations for the great bombing offensives of future years when Britain's most effective bomber, the Lancaster, became available. Victories were achieved against the Italian army in Africa in 1940, and against the Italian navy at Taranto in October 1940 and Matapan in March 1941. But Churchill's decision to divert a substantial force of Australian and New Zealand soldiers and a British armoured brigade to Greece was a major error which, once German forces became involved, resulted in a humiliating exodus from the Greek mainland and then defeat in Crete. This defeat also weakened the British position in North Africa.

The prospects of ultimate victory were transformed by two events which made first for a wider European war in June 1941, and second a world war in December 1941. The year 1940 has been seen as the fulcrum of the twentieth century, but perhaps 1941 has a better claim. Germany's invasion of the Soviet Union provided Britain with an incongruous ally and the USA's entry into the war was probably decisive in bringing eventual victory for the great new alliance in the long term (see Chapters 2, 3 and 4 of *The Second World War*). Comparisons of the economic and military potential of the Axis and Allied powers make it clear that the latter had the long-term advantage.

ACTIVITY

Briefly state what problems there were for Britain in allying with the Soviet Union, and why we have referred to that state as an 'incongruous ally'.

Spend no more than 15 minutes on this activity.

COMMENT

You may well have pointed to the enormous advantage that came with the Soviet Union's participation in the war. Here was a new and powerful 'continental sword'. But there were problems, and Germany's invasion of the Soviet Union necessitated a graceful (or graceless, according to taste) U-turn for the British government.

The state which had been seen as the equal in evil to Hitler's Germany, which had partitioned Poland with Germany, had swallowed up the Baltic States and invaded Finland was now an ally – the enemy's enemy had to be a friend. Arguably, having gone to war with Germany (at least ostensibly) because Germany had invaded Poland, Britain should have declared war on the Soviet Union in September 1939 when it invaded Poland. If Churchill's plan to come to the aid of Finland in early 1940 had come to anything, we would indeed have been at war with the Soviet Union. Hitler's fellow butcher, Stalin, was soon transformed into 'Uncle Joe', a benevolent figure. Some, like Evelyn Waugh's fictional Captain Guy Crouchback (see Waugh's trilogy, *Sword of Honour*), were ashamed. But Britain now had an ally and the British propaganda machine was determined that the Soviet Union should be seen as a gallant ally. And it was largely successful.

Of course this meant reneging on the Poles but there wasn't much choice. It was to be the strength of the Soviet army, which suffered enormous casualties, and the effectiveness of Russia's production of war materials that was to blunt Germany's war machine.

Nor was the USA's involvement in the war after Pearl Harbor a totally unmixed blessing, though blessing it undoubtedly was. The alliance of the two democratic powers was more natural than that with the Soviet Union, but the interests and aims of Britain and the USA were far from synonymous.

The wider war and the Grand Alliance can be seen to have marked the end of the war that was peculiarly Britain's war and retrospectively be seen as marking the point at which Britain began to lose its status as a great power. However, the credit side of this was considerable. Britain would survive and Germany would be defeated.

In the short term things did not look this way. The early months of 1942 saw German armies move deep into Soviet territory, while the surrender of General Percival and his army of British, Australian and Indian forces (which, while poorly trained and equipped, actually outnumbered the Japanese) at Singapore was the most humiliating defeat in the history of the British Empire.

The entry of Japan into the war brought about the nightmare scenario for Britain that Chamberlain had, at all costs, wished to avoid: a war in Europe and a war in the Far East. Britain would emerge on the winning side in both wars owing to Soviet and US assistance in the one war and US predominance in the other.

Figure 4 *Blimpapore*, 22 January, 1942 (*Source*: Low, *The World at War: A History in Sixty Cartoons with a Narrative Text*, Harmondsworth, Penguin, 1942, p. 115)

Neither certainty of eventual victory nor Britain's subordinate position was immediately apparent. It was not until late in 1944 that US forces were more numerous in the European theatre than British and, even then, Churchill's prestige and personality did much to ensure that there was a 'Big Three' – Roosevelt, Stalin and Churchill – rather than a 'Big Two'. The three war leaders shared the aim of defeating Germany but there were mutual suspicions: Stalin was suspicious that the British and Americans would conclude a separate peace with Germany, while Britain and the USA, with good reason, suspected that Stalin might do the same. (There can be little doubt that the Soviet Union and Germany considered peace deals from as early as 1942 until as late as 1944.) Nor can there be much doubt that President Roosevelt looked forward to a less powerful Britain – the end of the British Empire; the end of the Sterling Area; and the end of the Royal Navy's position as the most powerful navy in the world.

The future of the British Empire looked increasingly uncertain as the war progressed. As we have seen, it is difficult to exaggerate the importance of the empire to the Britain of 1939 or its importance to Britain's ability to defend itself and fight on after May 1940. Without the dominions, in particular, Britain would have been militarily much weaker. In the war against Japan, the continued loyalty of the Indian army was to be crucial, but, nevertheless, the successes of Japanese forces in 1941–4 dealt a great blow to the prestige of the empire and paved the way for demands for national independence, supported by the USA, after the war.

Throughout the war British and empire forces continued to make a major contribution to the allied cause from El Alamein in October 1942, through the landings in Sicily and the Italian mainland and the long haul up the Italian peninsula, to D-Day and the final push into Germany in 1945.

Victory over Japan was, nevertheless, undoubtedly due to US forces and weaponry while, as the US build up in Europe continued, however, Britain became increasingly the junior partner in the European war as well. It was the US General, General Eisenhower, who was given overall command of the allied forces in the Mediterranean before the invasion of Sicily. It was the US insistence on an invasion of France that prevailed over Churchill's preference for operations in Italy and the Aegean.

As the allied build up for the Normandy landings took place in the first half of 1944, US troops became ubiquitous in the south of England, where there were already numerous US air bases. But US troops weren't always popular. England and London in particular had become rather cosmopolitan during the war with the governments in exile of various countries and an assortment of Polish, Free French, Czech and other foreign forces mingling with troops from the Empire and Commonwealth. But US service personnel were particularly noticeable not just because of their numbers but because of their relative affluence and spending power. Their ignorance of British mores, the fact that they had plenty of cigarettes and chocolate, could get nylon stockings for girlfriends, and were far better paid than their British counterparts, did not endear them to British service personnel. A Mass-Observation poll (the organisation was getting more scientific), for instance, found that Londoners were far less favourable to Americans than to other allied troops. US troops were, nevertheless, undoubtedly popular with many young women. As one woman who grew up in Leamington Spa has recalled:

> I think we all thought they lived in huge houses with swimming pools and big cars, just like in the films, but they certainly were attractive because their uniforms were so much smarter than the English army outfits. They had that certain air about them too.

(BBC *WW2 People's War*, Eva Coad)

Perhaps there was also a realisation and a resentment that the USA was supplanting Britain. In retrospect the road to victory can, as we have seen, be also seen as marking the road to the end of Britain's position as a great power. Chamberlain's fears that a war would mean the end of the Empire, economic decline and a diminution of Britain's status were being realised. There was already the beginning of an odd sort of nostalgia for the heroic days of 1940–41.

A degree of war-weariness was understandable. Even after D-Day the war in Europe dragged on while an end to the war in the Far East seemed distant. Fear of invasion was a memory but if bombing raids were less prevalent there was new danger from the V1s, the 'doodlebugs' or 'buzz bombs', and V2s. Increasingly, attention was on the eagerly awaited end of the war and what it would bring.

As we have seen, from 1940 onwards there was considerable emphasis in the media not just on winning the war but on what sort of Britain was being fought for. Churchill was disinclined to spend too much time on the latter subject, feeling that too much discussion on how to improve society after the war was likely to raise false hopes and, in any case, it took people's minds off the task in hand, which was winning. With exceptions, it was the Conservative ministers who held the portfolios concerned with the prosecution of the war and the Labour ministers who held the domestic portfolios. The Beveridge Report (December 1942) has been seen as the blueprint for a future welfare state. The 1945 General Election, which gave Labour a large majority of seats, has often been seen as the result of the way in which the media had dwelt on social and economic matters during the war. Although it may well have had to do with a worry that Churchill, popular though he was, might take too strong a line against the Soviet Union and this could lead to another war.

When victory in Europe was declared, the crowds cheered outside Buckingham Palace, but Britain, even if victorious, was much weakened and the bills for the war would come in. In 1945, however, few British people seem to have thought too much about Britain's future place in the world. The overwhelming emotions were joy and relief that the war had come to an end.

ACTIVITY

Listen now to Item 14, 'The King on VJ Day', on your DVD. This speech was made to the British Empire on 15 August 1945, following the surrender of Japan.

BRITAIN AND WORLD WAR 2: THE DEBATE CONTINUES

We discuss the effects of the war on Britain on the DVD and you may find it useful to listen to the discussion to this discussion before reading any further.

ACTIVITY

Now listen to Item 15, 'Consequences', on your DVD.

A standard account of Britain's war accepted the heroic version of Britain's struggle, never questioning whether it was in the long-term national interest. This account, combined with a positive view of the impact of the war on British politics and society, prevailed, unassailed, for several decades after the war. Essentially this account accepted that: Chamberlain was wrong and Churchill was right; that the thirties were a dark decade; that Britain found its soul between 1940 and 1941; and that the Grand Alliance was a crusade against fascism (even if the Alliance was sundered by the Cold War). An addition to this account stated that the war produced the post-war Labour government, and saw the beginning of a supposedly beneficent consensus for a more generous and less class-conscious (if less powerful) Britain, in which the state would play a more interventionist role.

Since the late 1960s this narrative has come under attack from historians both of the left and the right. Chamberlain and Baldwin have been defended, while Churchill has been derided both for his mistakes as war supremo and for allowing Britain to become subordinate to the USA. Britain's 'finest hour' has been seen as a myth. The post-war reconstruction of Britain has been seen as either a self-indulgent fantasy which neglected economic reality or, alternatively, as reneging on a popular desire to turn Britain into a socialist state.

This discussion has examined many of these issues. We have concurred to some extent with Chamberlain's analysis of the disastrous effects war would have on Britain's economy, and on its world and imperial position. We have also agreed with those who both sympathise with Chamberlain's efforts to avoid war and recognise that the 1930s were far from the caricature of the 'Devil's Decade'.

The central question we have tried to involve you in addressing is the nature of what has been seen as Britain's 'finest hour', the period from June 1940 to June 1941. A number of historians have attacked the 'myths' of this period. Malcolm Smith's *Britain and 1940: History, Myth and Popular Memory* (2000) somewhat belies its title. If, to some extent, it debunks the hallowed version of the key period in Britain's war, it also argues that there can be no clear distinction between myth and fact. It argues that myths are necessary and that there can be no 'true' historical accounts.

Angus Calder in *The People's War: Britain 1939–45* (1969) and *The Myth of the Blitz* (1991) is partial in his demolition of the traditional account attacking its more conservative and patriotic aspects and making much of the supposed radicalisation of the people's war. He argues that this supposed radicalisation made the population eager for a new socialist Britain; their eagerness forged from the unity and communal feelings of 1940–41, enlivened by memories of the harsh conditions of pre-war Britain, and encouraged by alliance with the Soviet Union. Calder argues that this popular desire was betrayed by the Labour politicians and civil servants, who interpreted the mandate of the 1945 General Election to mean improving liberal capitalism rather than developing a socialist society.

From a different political point of view, more Conservative historians have questioned Churchill's understanding of Britain's long-term international interests and Labour's domestic policies. John Charmley in his *Churchill: The End of Glory* (1993) has depicted Churchill as little realising the price Britain would pay for the Grand Alliance in terms of loss of great power status. Corelli Barnett has argued in *The Audit of War: The Illusion and Reality of Britain as a Great Nation* (1987) that self-satisfaction in Britain's supposed heroic role and the glow of its eventual victory blinded governments to the major failings in wartime production and its strike-ridden record. This blindness resulted in the disastrous economic and social policies of the post-war Labour governments. These governments, while euphoric in victory, thought Britain could have the 'New Jerusalem' of the Welfare State, without modernising and supporting industrial production.

Much of the debate is, as you will have grasped, ideological and involves value judgements: Was Hitler worse than Stalin? How bad or good a society was Britain in the thirties? Did the British people fight for King and Country or the hope of a Welfare State? Was the Empire a good thing, even if it was important and popular? Was the war fought for the national interest or was it a war fought against fascism? We could go on.

It's obvious that the British people's view of the war determined their view of themselves after the war and, indeed, determines it in the present day. That's why history is so important. It influences our view of Europe and of the USA and of our place in the world.

As we have argued, a whiter than white account of Britain's war will not stand up. But then no historical account of any war could portray perfection; probably a few of the Spartan soldiers at Thermopylae wavered. Although we cannot rely just on oral testimony, the examples we have used do, for the most part, confirm a spirit of defiance and of national unity in the face of the threat of invasion. There is also evidence that Churchill was a charismatic and inspirational figure, whatever his failings as a strategist. But oral evidence does not present a strong case for the idea that a social agenda for a 'better Britain' was the main stimulus for patriotism and a defiance of Germany. People seem to have been content to fight and suffer for Britain as it was.

What comes home is a mixture of patriotism and cynicism. Yet a derisory view of politics and politicians – Churchill for the moment excepted – is not incompatible with patriotism.

An important criticism of Britain's war and its image is that it gave the British people a heroic image of themselves which was inappropriate for Britain's diminished post-war position. During the 1970s, when the British economy seemed to lag behind those of European states which had experienced defeat, it was alleged that Britain was too comfortable with itself and too conservative, due in part to pride in its past. Indeed, such views were aired soon after the war. Angus Calder in *The Myth of the Blitz* points to a little known Noel Coward play, *Peace in Our Time,* staged in London in 1947. It is set in an imaginary London five years after a successful German invasion; there has been a resistance movement and allied forces are now liberating Britain. In reply to the question as to whether it would have been better if we had won the Battle of Britain one character replies that it would not have been:

> Because we should have got lazy again, and blown out of our own glory. We should have been bombed and blitzed and we should have stood up under it – an example to the whole civilised world – and that would have finished us.

Was the Second World War a 'people's war'? This has been a major theme of our discussion in this Study Guide. We can define a 'people's war' in several ways: a people united in the war effort; a people finding a new communal solidarity; or a people determined to fight for a utopia. We would suggest that the British people, though not universally contented with their lot, fought for the Britain they knew and hoped to improve, but were suspicious of utopias. They hoped for a return to normality and privacy after the war was over, while many had come to believe that the state could help them realise their hopes. The results of the 1945 election have been much pondered over. The vagaries of the British electoral system gave Labour a big majority, though total votes were much closer. Did this give Labour a mandate for socialism, or had the electorate voted for a bit more welfare provision and a few more houses?

The comment that someone had a 'good war' usually meant that they had been promoted, achieved high rank, or been decorated. In a wider sense many people had good wars, enjoyable wars. But because so many people had bad wars – lost husbands, wives or parents in battle, air-raid or sunken ship, or suffered in captivity – this is a sensitive matter. It is, however, impossible to deny that for many people the war broadened their horizons, took them away from narrow lives, narrow roles, or boring jobs, and gave them exciting experiences. The war loosened social and (especially) sexual mores, for better or worse. Of course, people tend to remember the good times – the parties, the camaraderie, the boyfriends or girlfriends – and not the fear, danger and the boredom; not the meagre rations and the restrictions. Oral history reveals a lot of good wars as well as many tragic ones.

Britain had a good war in the sense that national pride was evident and justified in 1945. Neither leaders nor people had welcomed war and six years of sacrifice and hardship had followed. Few realised that the price of victory would be a less powerful and influential Britain. Even at the war's end, hardly anyone considered that the British Empire would soon fade away. In this sense, Britain had a bad war, although the economic, financial and strategic decline would not become evident for some years. There was a general expectation of a brighter future, but Britain was a pretty exhausted country that celebrated peace and cautiously removed the blackout curtains. Rationing and shortages were to continue in the rather threadbare and shabby Britain of the late 1940s.

To compare generations is an exercise fraught with difficulties but the testimony of a woman in the WAAF that:

> … Britain really was a different place back then. We really did all pull together for a common cause, endeavouring in our own small way to deliver the war back to a brutal tyranny that was attempting to enslave us.

(BBC *WW2 People's War,* Eileen Jones)

For all that historical revisionism has done to challenge the notion of a people's war, it is difficult to refute such a view of the war.

REFERENCES

Addison, P. (1975) *The Road to 1945: British Politics and the Second World War*, London, Jonathan Cape.

Aronson, Theo (1993) *The Royal Family at War,* London, John Murray.

Barnett, Corelli (1986) *The Audit of War: The Illusion and Reality of Britain as a Great Nation*, London, Macmillan.

Beveridge, W. (1942) *Report on Social Insurance and Allied Services*, London, HMSO.

Calder, A. (1969) *The People's War: Britain 1939–1945*, London, Jonathan Cape.

Calder, A. (1991) *The Myth of the Blitz*, London, Jonathan Cape.

Calder, A. and Sheridan, D. (1984) *Speak for Yourself*, Oxford, Oxford University Press.

Cato (1940), *Guilty Men*, London, Gollancz.

Charmley, John (1993) *Churchill: The End of Glory*, London, Hodder and Stoughton.

Documentary News Letter (1940) September.

Documentary News Letter (1941) February, July.

Donnelly, M. (1999) *Britain in the Second World War*, London, Routledge.

Greene, Graham (1999) 'The Lieutenant Died Last', in *The Last Word and Other Stories,* New York, Penguin Books.

Ivatt, Ian (2000) *Food for Thought: Wartime in Steyning*, Steyning Museum.

Jennings, Mary-Lou (ed.) (1982) *Humphrey Jennings: Film-maker, Painter, Poet*, London, British Film Institute.

Marwick, Arthur (1975) *War and Social Change in the Twentieth Century,* London, Macmillan.

Mosely, Leonard (1971) *Backs to the Wall*, London, Weidenfeld and Nicolson.

Priestley, J.B. (1934) *English Journey*, London, Heinemann.

Ray, J. (1996) *The Night Blitz, 1940–4*, Arms and Armour Press.

Sheridan, Dorothy (ed.) (1990) *Wartime Women: A Mass-Observation Anthology*, London, Mandarin.

Smith, Malcolm (2000) *Britain and 1940: History, Myth and Popular Memory*, London, Routledge.

Taylor, A.J.P. (1965) *English History 1914–1945,* Oxford, Oxford University Press.

Torday, Jane (1989) *Wish Me Luck As You Wave Me Goodbye*, Stocksfield, Spreddon Press.

Waugh, Evelyn (1942) *Put Out More Flags,* London, Chapman and Hall.

Waugh, Evelyn (1961, 1st publ. 1952) 'Sword of Honour Trilogy': *Men at Arms; Officers and Gentlemen; Unconditional Surrender,* London, Chapman and Hall.

Wright, Basil (1940) *Spectator*, 25 October.

Further reading list

Aldgate, Anthony and Richards, Jeffrey (1994) *Britain Can Take It: British Cinema in the Second World War* (2nd edn), Edinburgh, Edinburgh University Press.

Barnett, Corelli (1987) *The Audit of War. Illusion and Reality of Britain as a Great Nation*, Macmillan.

Calder, Angus (1969) *The People's War: Britain 1939–1945*, London, Jonathan Cape.

Calder, Angus (1991) *The Myth of the Blitz*, London, Jonathan Cape.

Chapman, James (1998) *The British at War: Cinema, State and Propaganda 1939–45*, I.B. Tauris.

Charmley, John (1993) *Churchill: The End of Glory*, London, Hodder and Stoughton.

Hayes, Nick and Hill, Jeff (eds) (1999), *'Millions Like Us'? British Culture in the Second World War*, Liverpool, Liverpool University Press.

Kee, Robert (1985), *1945: The World We Fought For*, London, Hamish Hamilton.

Mackay, Robert (2002) *Half the Battle: Civilian Morale in Britain during the Second World War*, Manchester, Manchester University Press.

Nicholas, Siân (1996) *The Echo of War: Home Front Propaganda and the Wartime BBC, 1939–45*, Manchester, Manchester University Press.

Ray, J. (1996) *The Night Blitz, 1940–4*, Arms and Armour Press.

ACKNOWLEDGEMENTS

Grateful acknowledgement is made to the following sources for permission to reproduce material in this product:

Extracts from stories which have appeared in this booklet and credited BBC *WW2 People's War* have been submitted to the BBC website of the same name. The copyright of these texts remains with the author; the right to reproduce them remains with the BBC. The BBC has a non-exclusive right to reproduce these. These extracts, or sections of them, should not be reproduced without prior permission of the BBC or the copyright owner.

Cover image:© Alamy Images

p.4: Open University; p.7: Film Images; p.12: Still from *The World Today*, 27 August 1936; p.17: Alamy Images; p.18: Solo Syndication; p.19: Still from *The World Today*, 27 August 1936; p.24: Imperial War Museum; p.25: Imperial War Museum; p.26: Solo Syndication; p.27: Alamy Images; p.34 Alamy Images; p.35: Still from *The Dawn Guard*, 1941, Film Images; p.44: Still from *London Can Take It!*, 1940, Royal Mail Film Archive; p.52: Still from *Millions Like Us*, 1943, Granada Media International; p.55: Solo Syndication; p.58: Solo Syndication; p.61: Alamy Images.

Studying with The Open University

We hope you have enjoyed learning more about 'The People's War' and that this study pack has given you an opportunity to try out studying with The Open University. If you are thinking about further study with The Open University, there are a number of ways of finding out about the courses we offer:
- visit our extensive website for the latest information about the wide range of courses and packs offered at all levels by The Open University: www.open.ac.uk
- email us at general-enquiries@open.ac.uk
- call us on +44 (0)1908 653 231
- write to the Course Information and Advice Centre, PO Box 724, The Open University, Milton Keynes MK7 6ZS, United Kingdom

To purchase a selection of Open University course materials:
- visit the webshop at www.ouw.co.uk, or
- contact Open University Worldwide, Michael Young Building, Walton Hall, Milton Keynes MK7 6AA, United Kingdom for a brochure
- tel.: +44 (0)1908 858 785
- fax: +44 (0)1908 858 787
- email: ouwenq@open.ac.uk